KU-263-748

ACC. No: 03174746

Major European Union Nations

Major European Union Nations

Austria
Belgium
Czech Republic
Denmark
France
Germany
Greece
Ireland

Italy
The Netherlands
Poland
Portugal
Spain
Sweden
United Kingdom

Major European Union Nations

SWEDEN

by
Heather Docalavich and Shaina C. Indovino

Mason Crest

Mason Crest
370 Reed Road, Broomall,
Pennsylvania 19008
www.masoncrest.com

Copyright © 2013 by Mason Crest, an imprint of National Highlights, Inc. All rights reserved. No part of this publication may be reproduced or transmitted in any form or by any means, electronic or mechanical, including photocopying, recording, taping, or any information storage and retrieval system, without permission from the publisher.

Printed in the Hashemite Kingdom of Jordan.

First printing
9 8 7 6 5 4 3 2 1

        Library of Congress Cataloging-in-Publication Data

Docalavich, Heather.
   Sweden / by Heather Docalavich and Shaina C. Indovino.
      p. cm. — (The European Union: political, social, and economic cooperation)
   Includes index.
   ISBN 978-1-4222-2260-7 (hardcover) — ISBN 978-1-4222-2231-7 (series hardcover) — ISBN 978-1-4222-9275-4 (ebook)
   1. Sweden—Juvenile literature. 2. European Union—Sweden—Juvenile literature. I. Indovino, Shaina Carmel. II. Title.
   DL609.D632 2012
   948.5—dc22
                        2010051848

Produced by Harding House Publishing Services, Inc.
www.hardinghousepages.com
Interior layout by Micaela Sanna.
Cover design by Torque Advertising + Design.

CONTENTS

SWEDEN
European Union Member since 1995

Kiruna

Gällivare

Boden

Piteå

Skellefteå

Umeå

Örnsköldsvik

Östersund
Härnösand
Sundsvall

Hudiksvall

Söderhamn

Gävle

Uppsala
Stockholm

Norrköping

Linköping

Borås

Göteborg

Helsingborg

Malmö

Introduction

Sixty years ago, Europe lay scarred from the battles of the Second World War. During the next several years, a plan began to take shape that would unite the countries of the European continent so that future wars would be inconceivable. On May 9, 1950, French Foreign Minister Robert Schuman issued a declaration calling on France, Germany, and other European countries to pool together their coal and steel production as "the first concrete foundation of a European federation." "Europe Day" is celebrated each year on May 9 to commemorate the beginning of the European Union (EU).

The EU consists of twenty-seven countries, spanning the continent from Ireland in the west to the border of Russia in the east. Eight of the ten most recently admitted EU member states are former communist regimes that were behind the Iron Curtain for most of the latter half of the twentieth century.

Any European country with a democratic government, a functioning market economy, respect for fundamental rights, and a government capable of implementing EU laws and policies may apply for membership. Bulgaria and Romania joined the EU in 2007. Croatia, Serbia, Turkey, Iceland, Montenegro, and Macedonia have also embarked on the road to EU membership.

While the EU began as an idea to ensure peace in Europe through interconnected economies, it has evolved into so much more today:

- Citizens can travel freely throughout most of the EU without carrying a passport and without stopping for border checks.

- EU citizens can live, work, study, and retire in another EU country if they wish.

- The euro, the single currency accepted throughout seventeen of the EU countries (with more to come), is one of the EU's most tangible achievements, facilitating commerce and making possible a single financial market that benefits both individuals and businesses.

- The EU ensures cooperation in the fight against cross-border crime and terrorism.

- The EU is spearheading world efforts to preserve the environment.

- As the world's largest trading bloc, the EU uses its influence to promote fair rules for world trade, ensuring that globalization also benefits the poorest countries.

- The EU is already the world's largest donor of humanitarian aid and development assistance, providing around 60 percent of global official development assistance to developing countries in 2011.

The EU is not a nation intended to replace existing nations. The EU is unique—its member countries have established common institutions to which they delegate some of their sovereignty so that decisions on matters of joint interest can be made democratically at the European level.

Europe is a continent with many different traditions and languages, but with shared values such as democracy, freedom, and social justice, cherished values well known to North Americans. Indeed, the EU motto is "United in Diversity."

Enjoy your reading. Take advantage of this chance to learn more about Europe and the EU!

Ambassador John Bruton,
Former EU President and Prime Minister of Ireland

Stockholm, Sweden's capital city

1 Modern Issues

Most people in Sweden are glad that their country is a member of the European Union (EU). When the Swedish Ministry for Foreign Affairs asked Swedes, "Do you think that it is positive or negative that Sweden is a member of the EU?" 44 percent of them responded that it was positive, while only 39 percent felt that it was negative. The remaining 17 percent replied that they did not know.

The Formation of the European Union

The EU is a confederation of European nations that continues to grow. All countries that enter the EU agree to follow common laws about foreign security policies. They also agree to cooperate on legal matters that go on within the EU. The European Council meets to discuss all international matters and make decisions about them. Each country's own concerns and interests are important, though. And apart from legal and financial issues, the EU tries to uphold values such as peace and solidarity, human dignity, freedom, and equality. All member countries remain autonomous. This means that they generally keep their own laws and regulations. The EU becomes involved only if there is an international issue or if a member country has violated the principles of the union.

The idea for a union among European nations was first mentioned after World War II. The war had devastated much of Europe, both physically and financially. In 1950, French foreign minister Robert Schuman suggested that France and West Germany combine their coal and steel industries under one authority. Both countries would have control over the industries. This would help them become more financially stable. It would also make war between the countries much more difficult. The idea was interesting to other European countries as well. In 1951, France, West Germany, Belgium, Luxembourg, the Netherlands, and Italy signed the Treaty of Paris, creating the European Coal and Steel Community. These six countries would become the core of the EU.

In 1957, these same countries signed the Treaties of Rome, creating the European Economic Community. This combined their economies into a single European economy. In 1965, the Merger Treaty brought together a number of these treaty organizations. The organizations were joined under a common banner, known as the European Community. Finally, in 1992, the Maastricht Treaty was signed. This treaty defined the European Union. It gave a framework for expanding the EU's political role, particularly in the area of foreign and security policy. It would also replace national currencies with the euro. The next year, the treaty went into effect. At that time, the member countries included the original six plus another six who had joined during the 1970s and '80s.

In the following years, the EU would take more steps to form a single market for its members. This would make joining the union even more of an advantage. Three more countries joined during the 1990s. Another twelve joined in the first decade of the twenty-first century. As of 2012, six countries were waiting to join the EU.

Obviously, though, opinions in Sweden are still mixed about the EU, even though the country has been an EU member since 1995. According to the same study, three out of five Swedes keep themselves educated about what the EU stands for and is working on. The most common sources of information are the daily newspapers and television news programs. About half of all Swedes think that information currently given on the EU functions well for them. Four of ten Swedes feel the need for more information. The Swedish people are well educated and highly literate, and although most people feel that EU membership has improved life in Sweden, there is still a sizeable minority that is unhappy with the level of independence Sweden has surrendered to the EU. In general, Swedes are distrustful of any EU measures that are perceived as a threat to Swedish *sovereignty*.

When Sweden first joined the EU, its people had a lot of concerns. The nation has a long history of *neutrality* during military conflicts; it also has many unique laws and customs. All this made the Swedes determined that EU membership would not override the wishes of the Swedish voting public. As a result, Sweden has established many areas where the country's own policies take **precedence** over those established by the European Union. There are several issues that concern Swedes, areas where they feel that their country and the EU may not be quite on the same page.

Some members of the EU feel that the European Union's laws regarding environmental protection and human rights are too **progressive**; these countries have a hard time complying with the standards set by the EU. In Sweden, however, the situation is just the opposite: Swedes are worried that the EU's laws are not progressive enough. When people in Sweden were asked what they thought the most important issue was that the EU ought to be the doing a better job

WHO HAS MORE POWER?

One of the big issues in the EU is similar to one that the United States faces as well: who should have more power, the central government (the EU in Europe, or Washington, D.C., in the United States) or the individual members (the nations of Europe or the states of the United States)?

The conflict between these two approaches often becomes more obvious when smaller issues arise. In the United States, it came to a head in the 1800s over the issue of slavery, causing the Civil War, but it continues to be an important question whenever states don't agree on a particular issue, such as same-sex marriage or abortion rights. The smaller issues in Europe are different (they often have to do with the rights of ethnic minorities, with the environment, and with money), but the big issue is very much the same. Will the EU be able to unite its power the way the United States did—or will it continue to act as many separate nations? That question still hasn't been settled.

Sweden has a reputation for being one of the most generous countries in the world in accepting refugees, like this young boy.

REFUGEES IN SWEDEN

When people flee their home country to escape war, famine, or oppression, they are known as refugees. Sweden accepts nearly 2,000 political refugees each year. The Swedish government is concerned, however, that the rest of the EU is not doing its share. The government has made this official statement regarding refugees:

"Sweden must take its share of the responsibility for the international protection of refugees. An important part of this responsibility is to provide protection—through resettlement in Sweden—for people fleeing in a third country who do not have access to any other permanent solution. Sweden is to engage in constructive cooperation with the UN Refugee Agency (UNHCR) and to have a humane refugee policy, as well as be a place of refuge for people fleeing persecution and oppression. The possibility of seeking asylum must be safeguarded and the trend in Europe towards more closed borders must be opposed. One of the Government's primary objectives in the area of migration is common asylum rules for countries in the EU. All EU Member States must share the responsibility for offering protection to refugees. If Sweden has to shoulder a disproportionate share of the responsibility for refugee situations around the world in relation to comparable countries, this will eventually raise questions about the sustainability of our asylum system."

addressing, the most common answer was environmental protection. Most Swedes also believed that the EU should be doing more to combat **hate crimes**—and they wanted EU member nations to take more responsibility for political refugees and to do more about gender equality issues.

Although Sweden is a full member of the EU, today it still keeps its policy of military neutrality. (In other words, during a war or military conflict, Sweden will not take sides or become involved.) This was a nonnegotiable Swedish condition during its membership process; it was simply too important to how Sweden views itself as a nation for its citizens to consider giving it up! However, Sweden does fully support the EU's conflict-pre-vention efforts, as well as its work to manage civil and military crises. Sweden is also willing to participate in European peacekeeping activities and **humanitarian** efforts.

When Sweden became an EU member, another important demand was that the country would not have to lower its environmental standards in areas where it had tighter laws than the EU. The outcome was that Sweden was allowed to keep its own laws while waiting for the EU to move closer to Swedish standards. Meanwhile, the EU has conducted a review of its environmental rules, including those for cadmium, arsenic, and various other chemicals, and it is working at making these stricter. Sweden is having a big influence on the rest of the EU!

Sweden also wanted to make sure the EU did not overlook the cold, sparsely populated areas of northern Europe because of how few people live there. Sweden insisted that the EU acknowledge the special needs of these people. The outcome was that the EU introduced a new type of regional aid for areas with population densities below 8 inhabitants per square kilometer. Almost half of Sweden is entitled to this special EU assistance. These funds have helped improve the **infrastructure** of many of the nation's most isolated and rural areas.

Like other EU countries, Sweden also has a number of traditions and customs it did not wish to

The company Systembolaget monopolizes alcohol sales in Sweden.

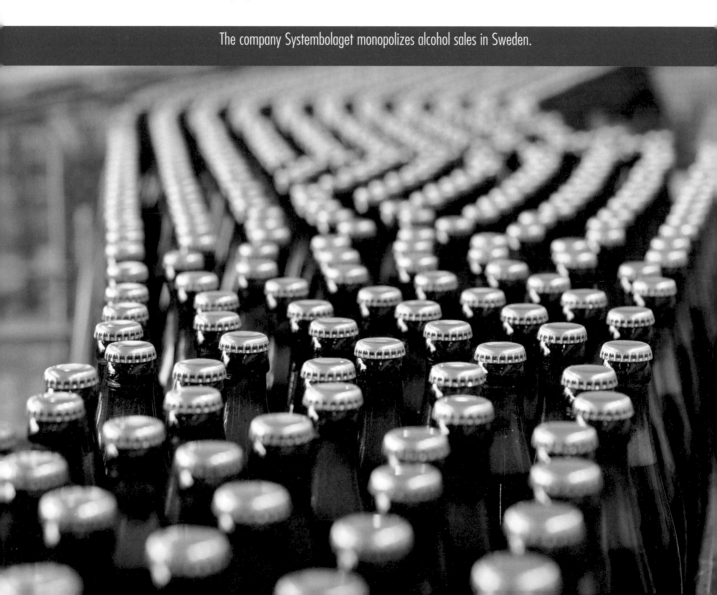

give up in order to join the EU. Many Swedes, for example, have a habit of using moist snuff (placing smokeless tobacco in the mouth); they were guaranteed the right to continue this practice, even though this product is banned in the other EU countries. Another issue that was important to Sweden during its EU membership negotiations was the right to continue operating Systembolaget, the government owned company that maintains a monopoly on retail sales of beer, wine, and liquor to the general public. Sweden persuaded the EU to allow the continuation of Systembolaget's retail monopoly. Today the importation of such alcoholic beverages is unrestricted, but they must be sold via Systembolaget.

This provision was actually challenged in the European Court of Justice in Luxembourg, which declared in its verdict that the monopoly did not violate EU rules. As long as it continues to stock a wide selection of alcoholic beverages and does not discriminate against any individual producer, Systembolaget may continue operating. The Swedes insist that the primary motive for the **monopoly** is for reasons of health, with alcoholic beverage sales thus being carefully controlled by Swedish law.

Most Swedes are proud to be a member of the EU—but they are even prouder to be Swedish. Their nation has a long, strong history that makes their land a special place.

Kalmar castle is a reminder of Sweden's history

2 SWEDEN'S HISTORY AND GOVERNMENT

CHAPTER

Sweden is an ancient nation that has existed as an independent and sovereign nation for hundreds of years. Signs of human habitation can be found in Sweden dating back to 9000 BCE. Sweden has a high concentration of ancient petroglyphs from that era that can be found all across the country. A petroglyph is an image carved by prehistoric peoples on natural rock surfaces. These images are thought to be the earliest form of nonwritten communication. The earliest images can be found in the northern province of Jämtland, and depict the hunting of wild animals such as elk, reindeer, bears, and seals.

SWEDEN IN THE IRON AGE

In the year 98, the Roman historian Tacitus described a tribe of people called the Suiones living on an island in the sea. These Suiones had ships that were noteworthy because of their distinctive shape with a prow on both ends. Today we recognize that shape as the classic Viking ship. The name *Suiones* refers to the peoples the Anglo-Saxons knew as *Sweons*, whose country was called Sweoland. In the epic *Beowulf*, this tribe is also called Sweoeod.

By the sixth century, the Ostrogoth historian Jordanes also wrote about the Suiones. Several

Seventeenth-century map of Sweden

independent historical sources mention a number of Swedish kings who lived during this period. At that time, kings were warlords rather than kings as we understand that title today, and their lands were a number of petty kingdoms whose borders changed constantly as the kings battled and killed each other. The politics of these early kingdoms are retold in *Beowulf* and the Norse sagas.

The period between 793 and 1066 is known as the Viking Age; this corresponds to the latter

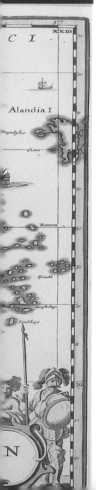

half of the Iron Age. During this period, the Vikings—warriors and traders from Sweden, Denmark, and Norway—raided and explored large parts of Europe, the Middle East, northern Africa, and even the coast of North America.

The longships used by the Vikings were the most technologically sophisticated of their day. Uniquely suited to both deep and shallow waters, these ships extended the reach of Norse raiders, traders, and settlers not only along coastlines, but also along the major rivers of Europe. The Viking leader Rurik founded the first Russian state with a capital at Novgorod. Other explorers from modern-day Sweden continued south on rivers to the Black Sea and went on to establish trade with Constantinople.

Swedish Vikings also played a role in Western Europe later in the Viking period. During the conquest of England under the Danish king Svein Forkbeard, Swedes, along with Norwegians, were recruited as ***mercenaries*** to aid in the invasion. Monuments in Sweden attest to the skills of warriors who returned home rich in plunder from English campaigns. Swedes were later recruited by the infamous Norwegian king Harald to help him regain control of Norway. These Swedish mercenaries subsequently helped Harald invade England in 1066, where he and his army were destroyed, marking the end of the Viking Age.

CHRISTIANIZATION AND THE EARLY SWEDISH KINGS

About the beginning of the tenth century, historical records note a king named Erik, whose kingdom seems to have reached as far as Norway. Later, another king named Björn is said to have been the son of Erik and to have reigned for fifty years. Björn's successors were his sons Olof and Eric, also known as Eric the Victorious. Following Olof's death, his son Styrbjörn was refused his share of power by Eric. Eventually, Styrbjörn attacked Eric, and a battle was fought between the two, during which Styrbjörn was defeated and killed. Eric himself died ten years after this battle, around 993. According to the story, he had obtained victory from the god Odin in return for a promise to give himself to the gods at the end of ten years.

Eric's son Olof succeeded him as king and instituted Christianity as the state religion. For the next 280 years, the land was ruled by a series of kings who gained and lost territory through long years of almost unending warfare. During this period, the newly Christian Swedes broke with the Roman Catholic Church and established the Church of Sweden. By 1275, the Swedish king, Magnus Ladulås found himself the leader of a heavily divided nation. Lesser rulers waged constant battles over small tracts of land, and the security of Swedish territory was threatened by enemies abroad who sought to take advantage of the country's instability.

King Magnus introduced a **feudal** system similar to that already established elsewhere in Europe, and as a result, the warring factions of Sweden were once more reunited. Magnus also promoted the formation of separate classes by extending the privileges of the clergy and instituting the **landed nobility**. Knights (lesser nobles and men of the upper middle class) now formed a heavily armed cavalry as the core of the national army. The period of Magnus's reign marks the rise of a prominent merchant class, as the towns now began to acquire charters. By the beginning of the fourteenth century, **codified** laws appeared, and the king and his council began to perform legislative functions.

Unfortunately, after the king's death, some of the instability returned as different nobles fought for the throne. The Swedes were briefly united with Norway in 1319, but various power struggles continued as a succession of kings were overthrown by their nephews and cousins. Eventually, at the request of the Swedish nobility, the Swedes formed an alliance with Queen Margaret of Denmark, becoming subjects of the Danish throne in what became known as the Kalmar Union.

The Kalmar Union

The Kalmar Union was formed by Queen Margaret I of Denmark in the Swedish town of Kalmar, then close to the Danish border. The Swedish king Albert, born in Germany, was disliked by the Swedish nobility, and their rebellion had received help from the Danes, who intended the union to serve as protection from the growing power of the Germans. As a result, Margaret united the three kingdoms of Denmark, Norway, and Sweden under a single monarch.

Eventually, the Swedes became unhappy with the Danes' frequent wars, which disturbed Swedish commerce. Also, the centralization of government in Denmark caused resentment. The Swedish nobility wanted to retain a substantial degree of self-government. The union began to dissolve in 1430, and ultimately, an armed rebellion led to the expulsion of Danish forces from Sweden. When the reigning king died childless in 1448, Sweden elected Charles VIII as their king, with the intent of reestablishing the union under a Swedish crown. Charles was elected king of Norway in the following year, but the counts of Holstein were more influential than the Swedes and the Norwegians together, and they made the Danes appoint Christian I of Oldenburg as king. The ensuing struggle for power

Sweden's stone fences mark ancient boundary lines.

The Royal Mounted Guard carry the pride of Sweden's history.

between Sweden and Denmark dominated the union for another seventy years.

The harsh policies of the Danes eventually led to the end of their rule over Sweden. After the bloody retaking of Sweden by Christian II in 1520 and the subsequent massacre of Swedish patriots, known as the Stockholm bloodbath, the Swedes started yet another revolt, which ousted the Danish forces once and for all in 1521. Independence was regained with the election of

King Gustav of the Vasa on June 6, 1523, restoring sovereignty for Sweden and finally dissolving the Kalmar Union.

THE RISE OF SWEDISH POWER

Gustav fought for an independent Sweden, crushing attempts to restore the Kalmar Union and laying the foundations of modern Sweden. At the same time, he broke with the Catholic Church. In 1517, Martin Luther, a German monk, led a revolt against the Roman Catholic Church. Lutheranism, the religious philosophy established by Luther, quickly gained a following across Europe. When the Roman Catholic Church supported the Danish king as the rightful ruler of Sweden, Gustav declared a split with Rome and appointed his own bishops to institute Lutheran reforms in the Church of Sweden. He also seized all Church holdings, thus stripping Rome of its wealth and influence in Sweden.

During the seventeenth century, Sweden emerged victorious in wars against Denmark-Norway, Russia, and Poland. Sweden, with about one million inhabitants, was beginning to emerge as a major European power. Following the Peace of Westphalia in 1648, Sweden ruled the Russian province of Ingria (in which Saint Petersburg later would be founded), Estonia, Livonia, and even some major coastal towns and other areas of northern Germany. By 1658, Sweden had also acquired important provinces in Denmark and Norway.

The increasing wealth and power of the Swedes did not go unnoticed by their neighbors. Russia, Poland, and Denmark-Norway formed a military alliance in 1700 and attacked the Swedish empire. Although the young Swedish king Charles XII won some important victories in the early years of the Great Northern War, his decision to attack Russia proved disastrous. With Swedish forces spread too thinly to adequately defend all fronts, the Swedes began to experience a series of defeats.

King Charles was killed during a battle in Norway in 1718. At the war's end, the allied powers, joined by Prussia and England, ended Sweden's brief period of glory by seizing her foreign holdings and introducing a fifty-year period of limited monarchy under parliamentary rule. In 1772, a bloodless *coup d'état* led by King Gustav III resulted in the return of *absolute monarchy*, a state of affairs that would last until limited monarchy returned following Sweden's involvement in the Napoleonic Wars of the nineteenth century.

Modernization of Sweden

The late nineteenth century was an important period of modernization and industrialization for Sweden. The nation's predominantly agricultural economy began to shift to a more industrialized economy. Unfortunately, wealth and prosperity did not increase at the same rate as the population. About one million Swedes immigrated to the United States between 1850 and 1890.

Many important developments occurred during this period, including the foundation of a modern free press, the abolition of trade monopolies in manufacturing to better promote free enterprise, the reform of national taxation and voting laws, the introduction of national military service, and the beginning of a multiparty political system. By the end of the century, three major political parties operated in Sweden: the Social Democrat Party, the Liberal Party, and the Conservative Party.

As the twentieth century dawned, the nation saw even greater changes. Industry continued to grow in importance to the national economy. **Suffrage** was expanded to include all men over the age of twenty-one, and sweeping labor reforms were made to improve working conditions in factories and limit the long hours worked by children. Sweden was once again growing in prosperity and influence when World War I swept across Europe.

World War I began on June 28, 1914, when Gavrilo Princip, a Serbian **nationalist**, assassinated Austrian archduke Franz Ferdinand and his wife, Sophie. Russia allied with Serbia. Germany sided with Austria and soon declared war on Russia. After France declared its support for Russia, Germany attacked France. German troops then invaded Belgium, a neutral country, as it stood between German forces and Paris. Great Britain eventually declared war on Germany. Soon the United States and other nations around the world were at war. Because of Sweden's out-of-the-way location, as well as the high demand on both sides for Swedish steel, ball bearings, wood pulp, and matches, Sweden was able not only to remain neutral throughout the conflict but also to profit from it.

The wealth Sweden accumulated during the war helped to buffer the effects of the worldwide depression that struck in the 1930s. During this period, the Swedes instituted many welfare policies regarding financial assistance for the unemployed, the disabled, and the elderly, which are the foundations of the modern **welfare state** seen in Sweden today.

Another result of World War I was the recognition by Sweden that declaring neutrality during a time of war was not necessarily a guarantee of escaping the conflict. Having seen the invasion

The royal crown and orbs

and occupation of other neutral territories during the war, Sweden began to invest in its military, determined to have the equipment and manpower to defend itself in case of foreign invasion. This proved to be very insightful planning.

WORLD WAR II AND SWEDEN TODAY

As Sweden increased its social welfare structure and military capabilities, the hardships faced in other parts of Europe that were devastated by the **Great Depression** caused great unrest. In Germany, the Nazi Party grew powerful, attracting members by offering radical solutions to the country's economic problems and upholding patriotic values. The Nazis' leader, Adolf Hitler, had ambitious plans for Germany's future.

Soon after being appointed *chancellor* in 1933, Adolf Hitler became a dictator. Hitler wanted to rebuild the German military power it

By the time World War II ended, Sweden had increased its airpower tenfold.

had lost in World War I. In 1936, he formed an alliance with Italy and signed an anticommunist agreement with Japan. These three powers became known as the Axis powers. France, Great Britain, and the countries that were allied with them became known simply as the Allies.

Hitler's stated goal of reclaiming German lands lost in World War I was initially accepted by the Allies, and a policy known as appeasement was developed that granted a series of concessions to Hitler in hopes of preventing another war. This ultimately proved unsuccessful, and Hitler's armies swept across Europe as World War II began.

Sweden once again proclaimed its neutrality in the conflict. However, Swedish policy during World War II had some distinct differences from the policies pursued during World War I. This time, the Swedes engaged in a policy known as armed neutrality. This meant that the draft was in effect, and all able-bodied soldiers were called to join the armed forces in case of foreign invasion. To pacify Nazi aggression, the Swedes allowed German troops to make use of a few railroads for transporting men and supplies, and Sweden continued to trade with both sides throughout the war.

The Swedish policy of armed neutrality may have been the only thing that saved the country from foreign invasion and occupation. The Germans considered invading Sweden because they coveted the nation's factories, natural resources, and ports. The Allies considered invading to establish a staging point for a further invasion of German-occupied Europe. In the end, both sides decided that the wiser course of action was to maintain trade and diplomatic relations and avoid armed conflict with the well-prepared Swedish forces. Sweden was able once again to avoid a conflict that devastated much of the wider world.

Following World War II, Sweden expanded its industrial sector to supply the rebuilding of Europe, leading to Sweden becoming one of the richest countries in the world by 1960. As a result of maintaining peace and neutrality for the entire twentieth century, Sweden has achieved an enviable standard of living. Governed under a social democratic system, Swedes enjoy the many advantages of a high-tech economy and extensive social welfare system. Because Swedes see their current prosperity as being directly linked to peace, the nation is still not a member of any military alliance. However, the country is anxious to maintain solid economic and political ties with its neighbors, which led Sweden to join the European Union (EU) in 1995. This move had economic as well as political implications for the nation.

A quiet street in Stockholm

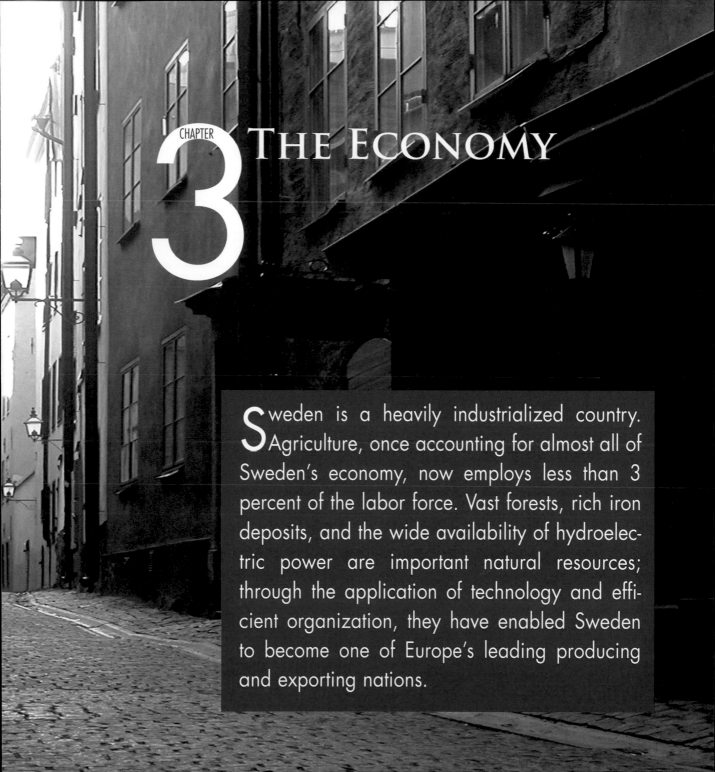

3 THE ECONOMY

Sweden is a heavily industrialized country. Agriculture, once accounting for almost all of Sweden's economy, now employs less than 3 percent of the labor force. Vast forests, rich iron deposits, and the wide availability of hydroelectric power are important natural resources; through the application of technology and efficient organization, they have enabled Sweden to become one of Europe's leading producing and exporting nations.

FORESTRY

Wood is Sweden's most important natural resource. The land is rich in timber, and many valuable coniferous softwoods are grown in Sweden, as well as a variety of less valuable hardwoods and several varieties of spruce and pine. The majority of Sweden's forests are privately owned by small farmers or form parts of larger estates, while a smaller area belongs to the state, the church, and local cooperatives. Major sawmilling and pulp corporations own the remainder of the forests. These corporate forests, which are among the best managed in the country, lie mainly in the sparsely populated north.

The annual harvest of timber in Sweden rose after World War II, from 34 million cubic meters in 1950 to 65 million cubic meters in 1971, then

Sightseeing in Stockholm

leveled off to around 52 million cubic meters in the late 1980s. Besides providing raw materials for manufacturing products such as paper, pulp, wood-fiber boards, and a wide range of chemical extracts, the forests are an important source of fuel and building materials. Jobs in lumbering, the transport of timber, and the wood-processing industries employ about a quarter of a million workers. The most important timber industry is the production of planks and boards. Its output reached a peak in the early twentieth century and has remained fairly stable since the 1930s. Sawmills are located in the small ports of the Gulf of Bothnia, particularly at the mouths of the Ljungan, Indals, and Ångerman rivers. The port of Sundsvall boasts the largest concentration of wood-processing plants in the world. Sawmills located on the northern shore of Lake Vänern export cut timber through the city of Göteborg.

Timber is converted into pulp either by grinding (mechanical pulp) or by boiling and solution (chemical pulp). About 70 percent of Sweden's pulp is now produced by chemical processes. The pulp industry is concentrated mainly in the ports of southern Norrland, especially around Örnsköldsvik, and on the northern shore of Lake Vänern, where Skogshall is an important center. Sweden produced 10.1 million metric tons of pulp in 1990. The most rapidly expanding branch of the industry produces sulfate pulp.

The paper industry is located mainly in central and southern Sweden, within reach of the shipping facilities of Göteborg and the national market in Stockholm for the newspaper and publishing industries. Norrköping and Halsta have important newsprint factories. Wrapping paper and cardboard are produced in the Göta Valley and on the northern shore of Lake Vänern. Sweden is the fourth-ranking producer of newsprint in the world.

MINING

The mining of iron and copper has been important to Sweden since the Middle Ages. An enormously rich copper mine at Falun in the Bergslagen region was mined continuously for more than 650 years, until it was almost exhausted. Sweden is among the top producers of iron ore in the world. Until the last quarter of the nineteenth century, the main iron mines were those in Bergslagen, but today the main source of iron ore is the remote northernmost part of Norrland. For the last century, the Norwegian ice-free port of Narvik has handled a majority of exports of Swedish ore. Swedish iron ores are extremely pure, with a phosphorus content of less than 0.3 percent. Bergslagen supplies most of the ore for iron and steel manufacturing. Its most important mining center, Grängesberg, supplies the integrated iron and steel plant at Oxelösund on the Baltic coast.

Sweden also ranks among the world's top copper producers. A new copper deposit was found in the early 1900s along the Skellefte River in Norrland. The main centers of copper mining are at Kristineberg, Boliden, and Adak, with some production still in Bergslagen. Sweden is rich in zinc, which comes from a number of sites in both the north and south. Nickel, lead, silver, and gold are also mined in Sweden. Large uranium deposits supply the nation's nuclear power industry.

INDUSTRY: THE MAINSTAY OF ECONOMY AND EXPORTS

Swedish manufacturing employs roughly 890,000 people. Metallurgy and engineering employ 48 percent of all manufacturing workers. The timber, pulp, and paper industries follow with 21 percent, the food and beverage industry with 9 percent, and the chemical industry with 8 percent.

The production of iron and steel is one of Sweden's vital industries. This industry is located mainly in Bergslagen. These modern iron and steel plants use the latest electrical smelting processes that eliminate some of the harmful by-products of past manufacturing processes. The largest iron and steel works is at Domnarvet. Two

QUICK FACTS: THE ECONOMY OF SWEDEN

Gross Domestic Product (GDP): US$379.4 billion (2011 est.)

GDP per capita: $40,600 (2011 est.)

Industries: iron and steel, precision equipment (bearings, radio and telephone parts, armaments), wood pulp and paper products, processed foods, motor vehicles

Agriculture: barley, wheat, sugar beets; meat, milk

Export commodities: machinery 35%, motor vehicles, paper products, pulp and wood, iron and steel products, chemicals

Export partners: Germany 10.5%, Norway 9.8%, UK 7.8%, Denmark 6.9%, Finland 6.5%, US 6.4%, Netherlands 5.2%, France 5.2%, Belgium 4.3% (2010)

Import commodities: machinery, petroleum and petroleum products, chemicals, motor vehicles, iron and steel; foodstuffs, clothing

Import partners: Germany 18.3%, Norway 8.5%, Denmark 8.3%, Netherlands 6.2%, UK 5.7%, Finland 5.4%, China 4.9%, Russia 4.9%, France 4.7% (2010)

Currency: Swedish krona (SEK)

Currency exchange rate: US$1 = 6.35 SEK (2011)

Note: All figures are from 2011 unless otherwise noted.
Source: www.cia.gov, 2012.

Stockholm's busy streets

large plants are also located near the coast, allowing the easy import of scrap metal, as well as the export of goods for engineering industries in other parts of Sweden and the port cities of northern Europe.

Engineering is the oldest and most highly developed manufacturing industry in Scandinavia. In Sweden, it accounts for about 40 percent of the total exports and produces a wide range of products, including machinery, tools, precision gauges, electrical generating equipment, ball bearings, automobiles, and military aircraft. Various engineering centers are scattered throughout the central lowlands between Stockholm and Göteborg.

The plants are often set in regional clusters, particularly around the shores of Lake Mälaren and in the Göta Valley. Malmö and the towns of southwestern Skåne are other important hubs of engineering industry.

Sweden was a dominant shipbuilding force for half a century, until this industry went into rapid decline in the late 1970s. A glut of ships on the world market (particularly of oil tankers), two international recessions, and fierce competition from low-wage countries like South Korea and Brazil have caused the total output of Swedish shipyards to fall dramatically.

AGRICULTURE

Agriculture has declined dramatically in importance in Sweden during the twentieth century. A basic feature of Swedish farming today is the widespread abandonment of land and the concentration of agriculture in the most favorable areas of the country. As small farms became deserted when their owners grew old and died, the government has intervened to compel the **amalgamation** of the property into larger units. Consequently, the number of small, privately owned farms has fallen since the 1950s.

Although only about 1 percent of the labor force held agricultural jobs in 2011, compared with 29 percent in 1940, agricultural output has not declined. In fact, modern technology has led to an increase in output despite the reduced area of farmland. Field drains, striking experiments in plant breeding for northern latitudes, widespread use of fertilizers, cooperatives for marketing agricultural commodities, and **dissemination** of technical information on farming have all contributed to increased harvests.

As in the other Scandinavian countries, the principal agricultural activity in Sweden is raising livestock. Because of the importance of livestock, three-quarters of the land under cultivation is devoted to fodder crops. More than half of this area is devoted to growing rotation grass, a fast-growing combination of rye grass, timothy, and clover. Most of this grass is converted into hay for the indoor feeding of livestock in winter, which lasts from five to seven months. Cereals are the second-most important crop. The main wheat-producing areas are the central lowlands and Skåne, though spring wheat is grown at favorable sites in Norrland's valleys as far north as the Arctic Circle. Rye and oats grow extensively on the western coastal plains. Barley is an important fodder crop in southwest Skåne.

Due to the long decline in its relative economic importance, Swedish government programs of price supports and incentives have sustained the country's agricultural sector. Swedish agricultural policy had as its goal the maintenance of an 80 percent level of self-sufficiency for farms providing basic foodstuffs. However, subsidies have been significantly cut back in recent years.

ENERGY SOURCES

In the 1960s and 1970s, the Swedish government devoted major resources to the development of its nuclear generating capacity, making Sweden, with

A busy restaurant in Stockholm

The world's largest ferries dock at Södermalm Pier

twelve nuclear power plants, by far the world's largest per capita producer of nuclear energy. A referendum in 1980 overwhelmingly endorsed phasing out nuclear power by 2010, but the plan was put on hold in 1990. Since then, the phase-out plan has been shelved; Sweden will now replace old reactors with new ones. Nuclear power provides about 40 percent of Sweden's electricity today.

Hydroelectric power has also played an important role in economic development throughout Scandinavia. Hydroelectric power plants provide Sweden with about half of its energy needs. Almost two-thirds of the country's hydroelectric potential has been utilized. However, for environmental reasons, no new rivers may be dammed unless alternative energy sources prove too expensive. The majority of the country's waterpower comes from long, powerful rivers in Norrland, while the chief area of consumption is in the cities of the central lowlands and the south. Thus, one of the main problems in the use of hydroelectric power has been the development of economical means of transmission over long distances.

TRANSPORTATION

Domestic freight in Sweden is moved mainly by road and rail. Trucks carry about half the nation's freight. State-built railroads are the principal means of commercial transport and carry one-third of the nation's freight and dominate long-distance hauling; they also move ores within the north. Shipping, chiefly of construction materials, accounts for about one-sixth of the freight. Sweden's merchant fleet was less than 4 million gross registered tons in 1980, and half that in 1990. Oil tankers accounted for about half the tonnage. Göteborg has the largest import trade, and Luleå the largest export trade. Sweden has a number of other ports of regional importance, including Stockholm, Malmö, and Norrköping. About 90 percent of the passenger traffic is by car and bus.

SWEDEN'S ECONOMY TODAY

In 2008, the United States economy entered a slowdown period. Many companies made less money or went out of business all together. As a result, there were fewer jobs, and unemployment soared. Because many people were out of work, they had less money to spend, which meant that businesses did even worse, creating a vicious circle that led to what **economists** call a recession. And because the economies of the world are so linked together, with nations trading with each other and many businesses operating in countries all around the world, the recession soon spread from the United States around the globe. As a result, the EU's economy also entered a recession—and so did Sweden.

From the early 1990s until 2008, Sweden had enjoyed a long period of economic strength that was fueled by strong exports and a rising demand within the country for goods and services. At the end of 2008, however, Sweden entered the recession that the rest of the world was already experiencing. Much of the Swedish economy was dependent on exporting cars, construction equipment, and telecommunication services—but now people and companies in the rest of the world no longer had as much money to buy the goods and services. Exports dropped, and Swedish companies were forced to slow down. During 2009, the **gross domestic product (GDP)** dropped by nearly 5 percent.

But the Swedish economy has bounced back faster than anyone expected it would. In 2010, the GDP grew by 5.5 percent, regaining the ground it had lost in 2009, and it continues to grow. Today, exports and investments are rapidly increasing, and the Swedish export market is expected to grow by 8 percent each year through 2013.

View of one of Sweden's banks in Stockholm.

Sweden has a strong, stable government that rules many areas of Swedish life, and the economy is no exception. Thanks to Swedish government policies, the Swedish national budget is always kept balanced. (The situation in the United States has been far different!) The Swedish budget process sets spending ceilings; these are promises that the government makes to its people—and keeps. This meant that when the economic crisis began in 2008, Sweden went in with a budget surplus.

This was a key factor that allowed Sweden to ride out the crisis better than most of the world's other countries. The Swedish Government released a conservative budget for 2011 aimed at reestablishing a surplus and consolidating the economic recovery. The budget contained new spending aimed at job creation, maintaining the welfare state, promoting exports, and tackling climate change. A series of additional reforms, such as lowering taxes on low- and middle-income earners, were also included.

One of the ways Sweden stimulates growth and raises revenue is through the sale of public assets. The government set a goal of selling some $31 billion in state assets between 2007 and 2010. Major sales have included selling V&S (Vin & Sprit AB) to French Pernod Ricard for some $8.3 billion, and the Swedish OMX stock exchange to Borse Dubai/Nasdaq for $318 million. Additionally, the government sold most of its 946 drugstores and eliminated its monopoly on pharmacies. The government has also approved the sale of Svensk Bilprovning (the Swedish Motor Vehicle Inspection Company).

The Swedish banking sector is made up of four large companies that account for about 80 percent of all banking activity in Sweden. The Swedish banks are heavily invested in the Baltic countries, which were some of the countries hardest hit during the financial crisis. Swedish banks suffered as a result; the government responded with a bank support package in 2008 that included guarantees for new debt insurance, increased deposit insurance, and a fund that would provide up to $6 billion in funds to be injected into vital organizations. In August 2010, the government revoked the license of one of the major Swedish banks because its business had become too risky. By taking these actions, the Swedish banking industry has remained strong. In 2010, all Swedish banks passed the EU's stress tests with flying colors. By this time, the economies of the Baltic nations were doing better as well, and Swedish banks heavily invested there began to grow once more.

Nevertheless, in 2011, Sweden's economy ran into troubles again. Although it continued to grow, its growth was much slower than experts had predicted. Still, a high-tech economy and a comprehensive system of welfare benefits give Sweden one of the highest standards of living in the world, allowing its people and culture to thrive.

Windsurfing in Stockholm

4 SWEDEN'S PEOPLE AND CULTURE

The population of Sweden was estimated at over 9 million in 2011. This gives the country an overall population density of fifty-seven persons per square mile (22 per square kilometer). Although Sweden as a whole is sparsely populated, regional population densities can vary greatly. The great majority of the population lives in the southern third of Sweden, especially in the central lowlands, the plains of Skåne, and coastal areas. Population is the densest around the cities of Stockholm, Göteborg, and Malmö. Large areas of the north are especially sparsely inhabited. Sweden is also highly urbanized, with more than 80 percent of Swedes living in the nation's cities.

Ethnically, Sweden consists mainly of Scandinavians of Germanic descent. Due to a dramatic increase in immigration, Sweden's ethnic diversity has grown rapidly in recent decades. For many years, Sweden was a nation of emigrants. From 1860 to World War I, more than one million Swedes left the country, mainly for the United States. Emigration declined significantly after 1930, as the nation grew more prosperous. Following World War II, Sweden welcomed many refugees and other displaced people. Since then, immigration has accounted for nearly half of Sweden's population growth. Today, approximately 20 percent of the population are immigrants or have at least one foreign-born parent. Many of these immigrants have come to Sweden as political refugees.

The largest immigrant groups in Sweden are from neighboring Scandinavian countries. About 17,000 ethnic Saami live mainly in the far north, although in recent decades many Saami have migrated south, mainly to Stockholm. Sweden is also home to large numbers of immigrants who fled the conflict in the former Yugoslavia, especially from Serbia and Montenegro, and Bosnia and Herzegovina. In fact, only Germany has received more refugees from that region. Other important immigrant groups include people from Iran, Iraq, Hungary, Turkey, and Poland.

RELIGION: FREEDOM OF CHOICE

The Swedish constitution guarantees freedom of religion. Approximately 80 percent of the population belongs to the Church of Sweden. It is possible to leave the Church of Sweden, and an increasing number of persons do so. In 1999, the Church of Sweden and the State separated, and, as a result, more than twice as many people left the church in that year as compared to previous years.

While weekly services in Christian houses of worship are usually poorly attended, a large number of persons observe major festivals of the church and prefer a religious ceremony to mark the turning points of life. Approximately 70 percent of children are baptized, 40 percent of those eligible are confirmed, and 90 percent of funeral services are performed under the auspices of the Church of Sweden. Approximately 60 percent of couples marrying choose a Church of Sweden ceremony.

Sweden has several smaller Christian faith communities as well. The Roman Catholic Church and the Russian Orthodox Church are represented. Several small churches are offshoots of nineteenth-century revival movements in the Church of Sweden. Others, such as the Baptist Union of Sweden and the Methodist Church of Sweden, trace their roots to British and North American Protestant movements.

The Jewish community has 10,000 active members; however, the total number of Jews living in the country is estimated to be approximately 20,000. There are Orthodox, Conservative, and Reform Jewish synagogues.

The major religious communities and the Church of Sweden are spread across the country. In recent decades, the large influx of immigrants has led to the introduction of nontraditional religions in their new communities. Islam is a growing religion in Sweden. The Muslim community has

Churches in Sweden are used primarily for ceremonies marking life's major events.

Twin-spired Växjö Cathedral in Småland

approximately 350,000 members; approximately 100,000 of those are active. Muslim affiliations represented by immigrant groups are predominantly the Shiite and Sunni branches of Islam. Buddhists and Hindus number approximately 3,000 to 4,000 persons each. The Church of Jesus Christ of Latter-day Saints (Mormons) and other foreign missionary groups are active throughout the country. Approximately 15 percent of the adult population is atheist.

FOOD AND DRINK: SMÖRGÅSBORD

Swedish food is usually simple and satisfying, and nowadays also healthy. In the last few decades, immigrants from all over the world have enriched their food culture with a host of exciting dishes. Foreign fast food has become an inseparable part of Swedish youth culture.

The feature of Swedish cuisine most familiar to foreigners is the smörgåsbord. Though the word *smörgås* means "open sandwich," and *bord* is the Swedish word for "table," a smörgåsbord is not a table full of sandwiches. Instead, this specialty consists of a number of small dishes from which you can take your pick. A typical smörgåsbord usually contains a number of herring dishes, Swedish meatballs,

QUICK FACTS: THE PEOPLE OF SWEDEN

Population: 9,103,788 (July 2012 est.)
Ethnic groups: indigenous population: Swedes with Finnish and Sami minorities; foreign-born or first-generation immigrants: Finns, Yugoslavs, Danes, Norwegians, Greeks, Turks
Age structure:
  0–14 years: 15.4%
  15–64 years: 64.8%
  65 years and over: 19.7%
Population growth rate: 0.168% (2012 est.)
Birth rate: 10.24 births/1,000 population (2012 est.)
Death rate: 10.21 deaths/1,000 population (July 2012 est.)
Migration rate: 1.65 migrant(s)/1,000 population (2012 est.)
Infant mortality rate: 2.74 deaths/1,000 live births
Life expectancy at birth:
  Total population: 81.18 years
  Male: 78.86 years
  Female: 83.63 years (2012 est.)
Total fertility rate: 1.67 children born/woman
Religions: Lutheran 87%, other (includes Roman Catholic, Orthodox, Baptist, Muslim, Jewish, and Buddhist) 13%
Languages: Swedish (official), small Sami- and Finnish-speaking minorities
Literacy rate: 99%

Note: All figures are from 2011 unless otherwise noted.
Source: www.cia.gov, 2012.

A typical Swedish meal includes salmon.

salmon, pies, salads, "Jansson's temptation" (sliced herring, potatoes, and onions baked in cream), eggs, bread, and some kind of potato dish. Smörgåsbord was originally served in the eighteenth century as an appetizer before the main course. Today, however, it has become a meal in itself. Few people ask for more after having tried everything on a smörgåsbord!

Kalmar castle on one of Sweden's lakes

5 SWEDEN'S FUTURE

Sweden prides itself on taking care of both its people and its land. Its strict laws are designed to ensure that the future will be safe and secure.

Social Welfare

Home to the world's highest tax burden, Sweden has created what is often called the world's most generous social welfare system, with such elements as virtually free (that is, tax-financed) education, child care, health care, pensions, elder care, social services, and various other social security systems.

Although Sweden has always had a solid **market economy**, the Social Democratic Party that ran the government for most of the twentieth century borrowed many ideas from **socialism**. Swedish wealth has been redistributed among the population to a greater extent than in perhaps any other country. "From each according to ability, to each according to needs" is the basic philosophy of socialism, which guarantees all people economic security in all stages of life.

The Swedish welfare state, known in Sweden as the "home of the people," is a unique experiment in social engineering that has attracted attention worldwide. In recent decades, however, the Swedish welfare state has been under heavy pressures. Today the country's social security systems are financially burdened and are struggling with serious structural problems. The recent flood of poor refugees and immigrants has increased the drain on the welfare system. Yet the main features of the Swedish welfare state, with its guaranteed and publicly financed safety net for the entire population, so far remain largely unchanged.

The Environment

The safety of the planet's future is of primary importance to Swedes. They understand that without the Earth, no economy would last long; if the Earth suffers, we will all suffer too. Because of this strong prevailing philosophy, the Swedish Parliament is aiming to solve all the country's major environmental problems within a single generation. The goal is to create a truly **sustainable** society. To do this, it has committed to fifteen objectives that are based on the following five fundamental principles:

- promotion of human health

- preservation of biological diversity

- preservation of cultural heritage assets

- preservation of long-term production capacity of ecosystems

- wise management of natural resources

The fifteen objectives are:

1. Reduced Climate Impact

2. Clean Air

3. Natural **Acidification** Only

4. A Non-Toxic Environment

5. A Protective Ozone Layer

Known for its environmental policies, Sweden protects its water sources.

6. A Safe Radiation Environment

7. Zero **Eutrophication**

8. Flourishing Lakes and Streams

9. Good-Quality Groundwater

10. A Balanced Marine Environment

11. Flourishing Coastal Areas and Archipelagos (islands)

Sweden works to protect the habitats of the animals which call the country home, such as this reindeer.

Sweden is proud of its beautiful scenery.

By making this commitment, Sweden is truly setting an example for the entire world.

Like any nation, Sweden faces many problems. But Sweden is determined to overcome them all!

Time Line

9000 BCE	Petroglyphs are carved by Sweden's earliest human inhabitants.
98 CE	The Roman historian Tacitus describes a tribe of peoples called the Suiones, now recognized as Swedes.
793	Vikings emerge as the dominant power in Sweden.
1066	King Harald is defeated while invading England, marking the end of the Viking Age.
1397	Sweden joins Denmark under the Kalmar Union.
1523	The Kalmar Union is dissolved.
1658	The Swedish Empire is at the height of its power.
1718	Sweden loses the Great Northern War. Her foreign holdings are seized, and a limited monarchy is established with the creation of the Riksdag.
1772	King Gustav reestablishes absolute monarchy.
1809	A new constitution is adopted.
1815	The Dutch monarchy is established.
1905	Norway officially separates from Sweden.
1914	World War I begins; Sweden remains neutral.
1917	Constitutional monarchy is founded on parliamentary democracy.
1921	Universal suffrage is given to men and women.
1939	World War II begins; Sweden remains neutral.
1946	Sweden joins the United Nations.
1960	Sweden becomes a founding member of EFTA.
1992	EEA agreement is signed.
1993	Sweden begins accession negotiations with the EU.
1995	Sweden joins the EU.
2008	Worldwide recession begins.
2009	Sweden's GDP decreases by nearly 5 percent.
2010	Sweden's economy bounces back from the recession.
2011-2012	Sweden's economy experiences a slowdown.

FIND OUT MORE

IN BOOKS

Furlong, Kate A., Kate A. Conley. *Sweden*. Edina, MN.: ABDO Publishing, 2002.
Thomas, Keltie. *Sweden, The Culture*. New York: Crabtree, 2003.
Thomas, Keltie. *Sweden, The Land*. New York: Crabtree, 2003.
Thomas, Keltie. Sweden, *The People*. New York: Crabtree, 2003.
Yanuck, Debbie L., Roland Thorstensson. *Many Cultures, One World: Sweden*. Mankato, MN.: Capstone Press, 2004.

ON THE INTERNET

Travel Information
www.lonelyplanet.com/destinations/europe/sweden/
www.travelnotes.org/Europe/sweden.htm

History and Geography
www.luth.se
www.sverigeturism.se/smorgasbord/ smorgasbord/society/history.html

Culture and Festivals
www.scandinavica.com

Economic and Political Information

www.cia.gov/cia/publications/factbook/index.html
www.wikipedia.org

EU Information

europa.eu.

Publisher's note:
The websites listed on this page were active at the time of publication. The publisher is not responsible for websites that have changed their addresses or discontinued operation since the date of publication. The publisher will review and update the website list upon each reprint.

GLOSSARY

absolute monarchy: A system of government where a king or queen has ultimate authority over the government.

acidification: The process of becoming more acid.

amalgamation: The process of combining two or more things.

chancellor: A head of government.

codified: Arranged into a systematic plan.

coup d'état: A sudden overthrow of the existing government, usually by a small group of people.

dissemination: The process of spreading something widely.

economists: Experts who study a nation or region's finances, jobs, and money system.

eutrophication: Excessive richness of nutrients in a lake or other body of water, frequently due to runoff from the land, which causes a dense growth of plant life.

feudal: Having to do with the dominant social system in medieval Europe, in which land granted by the Crown to the nobility was in turn held by vassals and worked by peasants, with each group owing homage and service to that above it.

Great Depression: The economic crisis that began with the U.S. stock market crash in 1929 and continuing through the 1930s.

gross domestic product (GDP): The total value of goods produced and services provided in a country during one year.

hate crimes: Acts of violence motivated by racial, sexual, or some other form of prejudice.

humanitarian: Concerned with or seeking to promote human well-being.

infrastructure: The basic physical and organizational structures and facilities (for example, buildings, roads, and power supplies) needed for the operation of a society or enterprise

landed nobility: The people whose land ownership guaranteed them the greater privileges of being considered a "noble" (rather than a "commoner").

market economy: An economy in which the prices of goods and services are determined in a free price system where the principles of supply and demand rule.

mercenaries: Professional soldiers hired to serve in a foreign army.

monopoly: The exclusive possession or control of the supply or trade in a commodity or service.

nationalist: Having to do with extreme feelings of love and devotion for one's country.

neutrality: A policy of not taking sides in a conflict.

precedence: A condition of greater importance or of coming first.

progressive: Willing to make changes and improvements.

socialism: A political and economic theory that advocates that the means of production, distribution, and exchange should be owned or regulated by the community as a whole.

sovereignty: The authority of a country to govern itself.

suffrage: The right to vote.

sustainable: Capable of being continued indefinitely with little long-term effect on the natural environment.

welfare state: A system whereby the government undertakes to protect the health and well-being of its citizens, especially those in financial or social need, by means of grants, pensions, and other benefits.

INDEX

PICTURE CREDITS

Pg 14 © turkishblue - Fotolia.com
Pg 16 © LE image - Fotolia.com
Pg 40 © Borodaev - Fotolia.com
Pg 53 © sanderstock - Fotolia.com
Pg 54 © Andreas Gradin - Fotolia.com
Pg 55 © sanderstock - Fotolia.com

All other images are from Corel image collections or are in the public domain. If any image has been inadvertently uncredited, please notify Harding House Publishing Services, Vestal, New York 13850, so that rectification can be made for future printings.

ABOUT THE AUTHORS

Heather Docalavich first developed an interest in the history and cultures of Europe through her work as a genealogy researcher. She currently resides in Hilton Head, South Carolina, with her four children.

Shaina Carmel Indovino is a writer and illustrator living in Nesconset, New York. She graduated from Binghamton University, where she received degrees in sociology and English. Shaina has enjoyed the opportunity to apply both of her fields of study to her writing, and she hopes readers will benefit from taking a look at the countries of the world through more than one perspective.

ABOUT THE SERIES CONSULTANT

Ambassador John Bruton served as Irish Prime Minister from 1994 until 1997. As prime minister, he helped turn Ireland's economy into one of the fastest-growing in the world. He was also involved in the Northern Ireland Peace Process, which led to the 1998 Good Friday Agreement. During his tenure as Ireland's prime minister, he also presided over the European Union presidency in 1996 and helped finalize the Stability and Growth Pact, which governs management of the euro. Before being named the European Commission Head of Delegation in the United States, he was a member of the convention that drafted the European Constitution, signed October 29, 2004.

The European Commission Delegation to the United States represents the interests of the European Union as a whole, much as ambassadors represent their countries' interests to the U.S. government. Matters coming under European Commission authority are negotiated between the commission and the U.S. administration.